Managing Editor
Karen J. Goldfluss, M.S. Ed.

Editor-in-Chief
Sharon Coan, M.S. Ed.

Illustrators
Howard Chaney
Bruce Hedges

Cover Artist
Lesley Palmer

Art Coordinator
Kevin Barnes

Art Director
CJae Froshay

Imaging
James Edward Grace
Rosa C. See

Product Manager
Phil Garcia

Publisher
Mary D. Smith, M.S. Ed.

Magnets & Electricity

SUPER SCIENCE ACTIVITIES

Written by Ruth M. Young, M.S. Ed.

Teacher Created Resources, Inc.
6421 Industry Way
Westminster, CA 92683
www.teachercreated.com

ISBN: 978-0-7439-3664-4

©*2002 Teacher Created Resources, Inc.*
Reprinted, 2009

Made in the U.S.A.

W9-DGK-795

Table of Contents

Introduction **3**
   Lesson: What Sticks to a Magnet? 4
   Lesson: Does One Magnet Stick to Another? 5
   Lesson: Magnetic Madness 6
   Lesson: Will Magnetism Pass Through Everything? 7
   Lesson: What Does the Magnetic Field Look Like? 8
   Lesson: Making a Picture of a Magnetic Field 10
   Lesson: What Happens When a Magnet Is Suspended? 12
   Lesson: Making a Compass 14
   Making a Magnet 16
   Lesson: Static Cling 17
   Parent Letter 18
   Lesson: The Magic of Static 19
   Particles and Electric Fields 20
   Answer Key 21
   Station 1: Popping Paper 22
   Station 2: Jumping Peanuts 23
   Station 3: Weird Water 24
   Station 4: Dancing Balloons 25
   Lesson: The Electron Dance 26
   Parts of an Atom 28

Light Bulbs and Batteries Lessons **29**
   Lesson: Can You Light the Light Bulb? 29
   Lesson: How Does a Light Bulb Work? 30
   Parts of a Light Bulb 31
   Lesson: Dissecting a Battery 32
   Cross Section of a Dry Cell Battery 33
   Will the Bulb Light? 34
   Lesson: Building a Flashlight 35

Electric Circuits Lessons **36**
   Lesson: Constructing an Electric Circuit 36
   Lesson: How Does a Circuit Work? 37
   Constructing Circuits 38
   Lesson: Inventing Circuits 39
   Will the Circuit Work? 40
   Lesson: Searching for Conductors 41
   Lesson: Mystery Connections 42
   Mystery Connections Record 44
   Electricity Assessment 45

Teacher and Student Resources **48**

Introduction

The activities in this book teach basic concepts of magnetism, static electricity, and current electricity through hands-on experiences. The sequential lessons lead to an understanding of the concepts and the relationship among all three areas. Throughout this series of activities, scientific terminology or vocabulary should not be emphasized. Instead, use terms your students can easily understand. For example, when working with magnets or static electricity, the scientific terms of *repel* and *attract* may be changed to "push" and "pull."

The study begins with activities in which students use a variety of magnets, such as bar, horseshoe, and circular, to discover their properties and reactions to each other. They continue using magnets to test through what material magnetism passes. The *invisible* magnetic field is outlined using iron filings to show its shape for single magnets and then for combinations of magnets. Finally, the magnetic poles of the earth are explored through the use of a hanging bar magnet to locate their directions from the classroom and finding the magnetic poles on a globe. The culminating activity for these lessons is to create a simple compass.

The study of static electricity follows with the first activity to charge balloons to demonstrate the effects of static electricity. Other static electricity investigations involve using Styrofoam pieces, paper circles from a hole punch, and flowing water. Students will use the same terms in this study as they did with their magnets. They also see that static electricity reacts just as magnetism does.

The final set of activities applies what students have learned thus far to the study of current electricity, using D cell batteries as a safe source of current. Students first discover how to make a flashlight bulb turn on using only one D battery and a thin wire. This leads to an understanding of the flow of electricity. Next, the light bulb itself is studied to find how this flow of energy from the battery makes the filament in the bulb glow. The logical next step is to create electric circuits and learn about parallel and series circuits. Students investigate what materials are conductors of electricity and discover that it passes through metal and water, just like magnets. However, unlike magnetism, they find electricity passes through different kinds of metals, not just those with iron in them. This study ends with mystery connection boxes that enable students to find the route of electrical current through a maze of wires.

Encourage the students to try the magnet and static electricity activities at home with their families. It may be possible to send home some of the equipment necessary to do the current electricity activities as well. By doing these at home, students learn more and have the delightful experience of teaching others.

What Sticks to a Magnet?

Teacher Information

Magnets will stick only to items which have *iron*, *cobalt*, or *nickel* in them. Cobalt and nickel are rarely used in common metal items; therefore, most objects which stick to magnets contain iron.

Overview: *Students will test various materials to tell what can be picked up by a magnet.*

Materials

- circular magnet with a hole in the center for each student (See page 48 for resources.)
- assorted small objects of wood, paper, glass, cork, various metals (including coins)
- *optional:* samples of magnetite and metallic rocks such as galena and pyrite (See page 48 for resources.)

Lesson Preparation

- Divide the materials into eight containers, each holding samples of the same materials.

Activity

1. Ask students where they have seen magnets used. Let them share these ideas in small groups.
2. Ask what they know about magnets, listing ideas on the board.
3. Divide students into eight groups and provide them with the containers of materials.
4. Have students divide the objects into three piles. One pile should be items which they think will stick to a magnet, a second pile is for those which they think will not, and the third pile is for items about which they are not sure.
5. After students divide all items into the three piles, ask them to tell how they decided which would stick to a magnet. (*Most will say that they chose anything metal for the "yes" pile.*)
6. List the items on the board under the three headings—**Yes**, **No**, and **?**. There will be some disagreement among the groups. List those items in question under more than one heading.
7. Distribute a magnet to each student to check the objects, placing them in new piles.
8. Discuss what they discover and change the objects on the board to classify them correctly.
9. Ask students if all metal objects stick to magnets. (*Very few stick—not even the nickels. Items of gold or silver will not stick to magnets either, even though they are metal.*)

Closure

- Let the students move around the classroom to test as many objects as they can to see if they will stick to their magnets (*most do not*). Do not permit them near computers for this test.
- Have them share some of the unusual items to which their magnets will stick. (If you have a ceramic sink in the classroom and the magnet sticks to it, it is cast iron coated with ceramic.)
- Tell students to find three places in their homes where magnets are in use and report this to the class the next day. Urge them to find magnets which are not very obvious. (Remind students to not place magnets near computers.)

Does One Magnet Stick to Another?

Teacher Information

Magnets have two poles which are designated *north* (positive) and *south* (negative). Opposite poles of two magnets will *attract*; poles which are the same will *repel* each other. Use simple terms with younger students when referring to names of the magnetic poles, as well as their reactions. Students can more easily comprehend north and south than positive and negative when talking about magnetic poles. Using *push* and *pull* to describe the repelling and attracting forces may be wise at first, since that describes what they will feel. Use the terms repel and attract when, or if, they are ready for them. It is important that they understand the concept, not the terminology.

Overview: *Students will learn about repelling and attracting forces of magnets.*

Materials

- circular magnet with a hole in the center for each student (used in previous lesson)
- wooden skewers which will fit through the hole in the magnets

Activity

1. Ask students the results of homework on finding magnets in use around their homes. Then distribute a circular-shaped magnet to each student.
2. Divide the students into small groups and let them "play" with the magnets. This will let them discover the magnets' properties. Allow at least ten minutes for this. Let the students learn through their own investigations rather than giving them information.
3. After they have investigated their magnets, encourage each group to share what they discovered and demonstrate some of their findings to the class.
4. Distribute a wooden skewer to each group and have them stack their magnets on it. Ask them what they find. (*When two magnets are placed on the skewer, they will stick or push apart.*)
5. Ask each group to stack the magnets on the skewer so they all push away from the each other. Let them discover how this can be done. Have them push down on the stack of circular magnets to feel the force between them. Explain that this is called a *magnetic force* and it is invisible. Tell older students when the magnets push apart they are *repelling*. Write the term on the board.
6. Have students rearrange stacking so all magnets attract each other. Let them feel the force by trying to pull the magnets apart. Introduce the term *attraction* to older students.

Closure

- Ask students to pretend each hand is a magnet. Have them show you the repelling and attracting forces with their hands by pushing them apart and pulling them together.
- Have the students make drawings of two magnets to show them pushing (repelling) apart. Let them make other drawings to illustrate two magnets pulling (attracting) together.

Magnetic Madness

Teacher Information

Poles are at the ends of bar and horseshoe magnets and on either side of rectangular or circular magnets. Magnetic poles will shift in magnets which are stored improperly. Bar magnets should be laid flat, side by side with opposite poles together. A steel "keeper" is needed to join each pair at both ends to keep the magnetic field from drifting. Keepers usually come with new bar magnets, but steel nails will work. Lay horseshoe magnets in pairs with opposite poles touching. Stack circular or rectangular magnets with opposite poles together. Marble magnets may be stored in circles in an aluminum pie pan or kept in the original plastic container.

Overview: *Students will investigate a variety of magnets.*

Materials

- variety of magnet types and sizes (e.g., horseshoe, circular, bar, and magnetic marbles)
- paper clips and 10-inch (25 cm) pieces of string

Lesson Preparation

- Place the magnets in containers to be distributed to groups of students and then exchanged. Tape to each container a list of the magnets in it. This list can be quickly checked when all are returned.

Activity

1. Review what was learned in previous lessons about the properties of magnets.
2. Divide students into groups and distribute a container of magnets to each. Let students investigate the repelling and attracting forces of all magnets. Magnetic marbles are especially exciting. (**Note:** After students work with the marbles, pry one open to show the cylindrical magnet inside the plastic sphere. This magnet is like a bar magnet with north and south poles.)
3. After students investigate their magnets, distribute ten paper clips and a piece of string to each group. Let them use these with the magnets to investigate further.
4. Challenge students to find the strongest magnet in their collection. Ask them to lay out the magnets in order of strongest to weakest. Now, tell them to test their magnets to see if they put them in the right order. (**Note:** This can be done in a variety of ways. Students can see how many paper clips each magnet can hold or can tie a paper clip to the string and find out which magnet can attract it from the greatest distance.)

Closure

- Have each group show their strongest magnet and how they proved its strength. (They may be surprised to learn that the largest magnet in their collection may not be the strongest.)
- Send home a note to parents, requesting that they lend magnets which they may have at home to the students for this study.

Will Magnetism Pass Through Everything?

Teacher Information

Magnetism is a strong force that passes through most materials, including air, water, paper, metal, wood, skin, bone, and glass. If a magnet is placed near iron or steel, however, the metal becomes temporarily magnetized and prevents the magnetism from passing through.

Overview: *Students will experiment to see if magnetism will pass through a variety of materials and thicknesses.*

Materials

- circular magnets
- strong magnets like cow magnets (see Resources section) or ones from a speaker or engine
- clear 9-oz. (270 mL) plastic tumblers half full of water

- paper clips
- 10-inch (25.4 cm) lengths of string
- items to test: cardboard, thin paperback books, aluminum foil or pie pans, wood (ruler or desktop), metal soup cans

Activity

1. Write on the board: "Can magnetism pass through water, plastic, glass, air, paper, metal, wood, skin and bone?" (Do not suggest answers but let students design their own tests.)
2. Divide students into eight groups and distribute magnets, cups of water, paper clips, string, and the items to be tested.
3. Let students use the magnets and materials they have received to answer the question.

Possible Methods: *The students can use their own hands to find if magnetism passes through skin and bone. The classroom window can be used to test glass. They can use the string tied to a paper clip and held a distance from the magnet to demonstrate the magnetic field travels through the air to attract it. Drop the paper clip into the cup of water and lower the magnet into the water. It should not touch the paper clip but be held above it to show that the magnetic force travels through the water.*

Closure

Ask the students if they found anything that could stop the magnetic field. (All items tested should let magnetism pass, except the tin can which has iron in it.)

- Let them demonstrate their tests to the rest of the class.
- If you have a powerful magnet, have a seated student place it beneath a thigh. Dangle a paper clip from a string above the thigh. The paper clip will be attracted to the magnet so that the string can be held at an angle rather than perpendicular to the leg. This will demonstrate that magnetism passes through the leg. Ask students if they can feel anything when the paper clip connects to the magnetic field. (*No, the magnetic field cannot be detected by the senses.*)

What Does the Magnetic Field Look Like?

Overview: *Students will see the magnetic fields of magnets.*

Materials

- iron filings (See page 48 for resources.)
- variety of magnets including circular, bar, and horseshoe
- pieces of 5" x 8" (13 cm x 20 cm) thin cardboard
- small jars such as used for baby food
- old nylon pantyhose
- rubber bands
- 8 ½" x 11" (22 cm x 28 cm) piece of glass (may be from a picture frame)
- overhead projector
- aluminum pie pans

Lesson Preparation

- Make iron filing shakers by pouring about five tablespoons of iron filings into each baby-food jar. Stretch a piece of nylon stocking over the top and fasten with a rubber band.
- Practice before doing the demonstration for the students.

Demonstration

- Ask the students if they can smell, hear, taste, feel, or see the magnetic field. (*They cannot directly sense the magnetic field.*)
- Ask them if they have ever dropped a magnet into sand and seen tiny black pieces sticking to it.
- Tell students you are going to make the magnetic field visible for them, using these iron filings.
- Place a bar magnet on an overhead projector and cover it with a piece of glass. (Support the glass above the magnet using lumps of clay, pencil erasers, or additional magnets under the corners.)
- Gently shake the iron filings through the nylon mesh over the area of the magnet beneath the glass. The bar magnet and magnetic field surrounding it will be outlined with iron filings.
- Dump the filings onto a piece of paper. Place the horseshoe magnet beneath the glass. Sprinkle the filings over the horseshoe magnet to outline its magnetic field. Repeat this with a circular magnet.

What Does the Magnetic Field Look Like?

(cont.)

Demonstration *(cont.)*

- Place two magnets (e.g., bar or circular) on the overhead stage so they will repel each other. Hold them in place with clay so they are separated but are still repelling one another. Place the glass sheet over them and sprinkle iron filings between them to outline the magnetic field. The filings will arc away from the ends of the magnets, showing the repelling force.

- Turn one of the magnets over so the magnets are now attracting. Hold them in place with clay and put the glass over them. Ask students to predict what the pattern of filings will look like between the magnets. Sprinkle the iron filings over them. The filings will form arcs between the ends of the magnets, showing the attracting force.

Activity

1. Divide the students into eight groups and distribute magnets, a jar of iron filings, a piece of cardboard, aluminum pie pan, and a piece of newsprint to each group.

2. Tell the students to place their magnets in the pie pan, using just one magnet at first. They should put the cardboard over the magnet. One student should sprinkle iron filings over the cardboard and see the magnetic field outline which results.

3. Caution the students to keep the iron filings away from the magnet. Have them always dump the filings onto a piece of paper placed far away from the magnets.

4. Let students investigate different magnetic field patterns, using various magnets in repelling and attracting positions.

Closure

- Have students use the equipment and the overhead projector to demonstrate some of the interesting patterns they discovered.

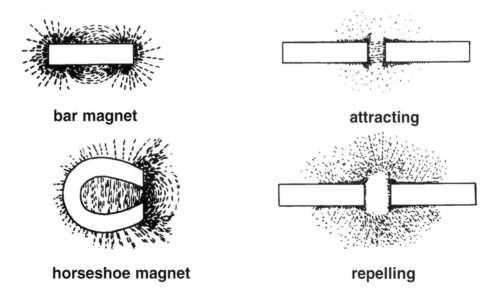

bar magnet

attracting

horseshoe magnet

repelling

Making a Picture of a Magnetic Field

Teacher Information

Paper impregnated with a chemical which makes it sensitive to sunlight can be used to make prints of the patterns created when iron filings outline magnetic fields. This paper is safe and easy to use and creates a permanent record of the magnetic fields outlined by iron filings. This lesson must be done on a windless, sunny day. The students will create designs in the classroom and carry them out into the sunlight so the sun can bleach the paper, leaving the print of the iron-filing shadows.

Overview: *Students will make permanent pictures of various magnetic fields.*

Materials

- sun-sensitive paper (available from Delta Education in Resources section)
- assorted magnets, aluminum pie pan, and cardboard used in previous lesson
- iron filings in jars
- dishpan filled with water
- pieces of newspaper

Lesson Preparation

- Make sun prints of a variety of magnetic field patterns as models for the students:

  1. Place the magnet(s) in the aluminum pie pan, covering them with the cardboard and adding a piece of sun-sensitive paper, blue side up, over the cardboard.

  2. Sprinkle the iron over the blue side of the sun-sensitive paper to create a clear pattern. If necessary, dump off the filings and try again until a clear pattern appears.

  3. Once the pattern is ready, carefully carry the setup, including the magnet(s), outside and place it in full sunlight. Let the pattern sit in sunlight until the paper around the iron filings has faded nearly white. This may take 5–7 minutes on a sunny day if the sun is high.

  4. Carry the setup inside and dump the iron filings off the paper. Place the paper into the pan of water which will fix the pattern, creating a white image of the area covered by filings.

  5. Once the white image appears, remove the paper from the water and place it on newspaper. Place another newspaper over the prints and weigh them down with books to keep the paper flat as it dries. After about 20 minutes, the books may be removed and the paper left to finish drying.

  6. Create a frame for the magnetic field pattern. Frames can be made using black paper larger than the sun-sensitive paper by at least 1" (2.54 cm) on all sides. Place cardboard the size of the sun-sensitive paper in the center of the black paper. Fold the paper around the cardboard edges and pinch the four corners of the paper so they stand up to form a frame. Glue the magnetic field print inside the frame.

Making a Picture of a Magnetic Field *(cont.)*

Activity

1. Tell students that they will be making a print of the magnetic field patterns using a special paper that will fade in the sunlight except where the iron filings cover the paper. Show them a sample of the magnetic field pattern(s) you made so they get an idea of what it will look like when they finish.

2. Divide students into small groups and distribute the materials used in the last lesson. Let them re-create some of their magnetic field patterns with the iron filings as a review of the process. After they have practiced making several patterns, let each group create one they will use for their print.

3. Distribute a piece of sun-sensitive paper to each student. Have them turn it blue side down and write their names on the back. They should keep the paper with the blue side down to avoid bleaching it from the light entering the classroom. One person from each group should set up the magnetic field pattern, this time placing the sun-sensitive paper on top of the cardboard. They need to be sure the blue side is up and that they sprinkle the iron filings over the sun-sensitive paper. The pattern will look exactly like the one they make with the filings.

4. Once the magnetic pattern is finished, students should carry pie pans with magnet(s), cardboards, and sun-sensitive paper outside to expose it to the sun. This is a critical time since once the sun shines on the paper it will begin to fade it. The paper should therefore stay as still as possible so filings are not moved. The pie pan should be laid in the sun, perhaps on a table to avoid having to lean and possibly shake the filings. Students should remain with the paper until it fades to white.

5. Students should return to the classroom as each paper fades sufficiently, dump off the iron filings, and then leave it in water until colors are set. The paper should be laid between layers of newspapers and pressed flat with a book.

Closure

- The finished product can be mounted on a frame of construction paper.

- Mount the pictures on a bulletin board and let students compare them. Have them identify the pictures which show repelling and attracting magnetic fields.

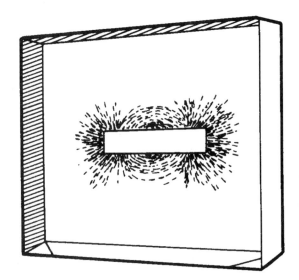

What Happens When a Magnet Is Suspended ?

Teacher Information

There are actually two north and two south poles on Earth. As Earth spins on its axis, one spot called the North Pole appears to point to the same point in the sky—the North Star or Polaris. The second "north pole" is located nearby at approximately 80 degrees north latitude and 105 degrees longitude in northern Canada. This is the location of the north magnetic pole. Earth's magnetic field acts as if there is a bar magnet inside it, with the north magnetic pole near the north geographic pole, and a south magnetic pole near the south geographic pole. The force is so strong it will pull on a freely suspended magnet which is not near any sources of iron. The suspended magnet's north pole points to the north magnetic pole and the south pole points to the south magnetic pole. This seems to contradict the rule of opposite poles attracting, so in this case the north pole of the magnet is referred to as the north-seeking pole.

Overview: *Students will learn about Earth's magnetic field.*

Materials

- strong bar magnet or cow magnet (See page 48 for resources.)
- string
- globe showing locations of the north and south magnetic poles
- circular magnets
- small white self-adhesive dots (*optional: small pieces of masking tape*)

Lesson Preparation

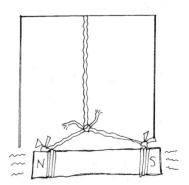

- Make a harness from the string for the magnet as shown.
- Suspend it from the classroom ceiling away from metal items.
- Balance the magnet in its harness so it is parallel to the floor.
- Let it swing freely; it should come to rest in a north-south direction.
- Test the magnet by tapping it and watching it swing. It should gradually come to rest in the same north-south direction.
- Place a piece of masking tape on each side of the "north-seeking" end of the magnet. You have just constructed a compass; the magnet is the compass needle.

Demonstration

- Show students the suspended magnet and have them notice the direction it is pointing at rest. They should see the tape at one end and use this as a reference point. Do not tell them this is the north end of the magnet.
- Tap the magnet gently to set it spinning and tell the students they need to watch it until it stops.
- As the spinning slows, point out that it appears that some invisible force is tugging it to stop.
- When the magnet comes to a complete stop, show that it is pointing the same direction as it was before. Ask students if they can explain why this is happening. Most will not be able to explain the reason, but some may guess it is pointing north-south.

What Happens When a Magnet Is Suspended ? *(cont.)*

Activity

1. Divide the students into groups and give each a circular magnet and a string about 10" (25 cm) long. Have them tie the string through the hole of their circular magnet.

2. Take the students outside to an area where there are trees low enough for them to reach the branches. Be sure the magnets are not within four feet of each other and that there is no wind blowing.

3. Hang the bar magnet from one of the branches also, away from the other magnets.

4. Demonstrate with the bar magnet how the students should gently twist their magnet around about five times to wind the string and then let it go so the magnet can swing freely.

5. Have them watch their magnets until they stop. Let them compare the positions of all the magnets (they should all be pointing in the same general direction). Have them look at the bar magnet and see what direction it is pointing. It should be lined up with their circular magnets.

6. Give each group a self-adhesive dot (or masking tape) and have them apply it to the side of the circle which is facing north, the same direction the north-seeking pole on the bar magnet is pointing.

7. Let them twist the magnets around on the strings again and watch to see if they stop in the same position. They have just identified the north-seeking pole on their magnets.

Closure

- Return to the classroom and show the students the globe and the location of the magnetic poles on the globe. Tell them about Earth's magnetic field and explain that it is so strong that it is able to pull their magnets in the north-south direction.

- Explain that if they could put a huge piece of glass over the earth and sprinkle iron filings on it, they would see the pattern of the bar magnet they used in the last lesson. The iron filings would form a huge arc from the north magnetic pole to the south magnetic pole. This magnetic field completely encircles Earth, and the zones of charged particles spread along the lines of that field are known as *Van Allen belts*, named for the scientist who suggested their existence.

North Magnetic Pole

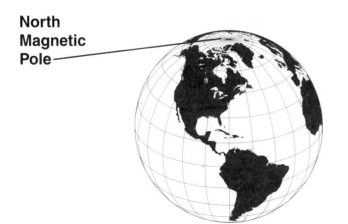 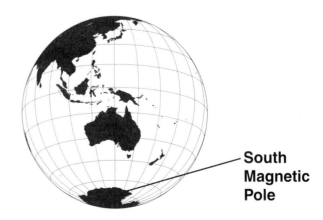

South Magnetic Pole

Making a Compass

Teacher Information

A natural magnetic rock was discovered long ago in the Greek province of Magnesia. The rock was named *magnetite* for the place in which it was found. Later, someone discovered that magnetite could be used to magnetize iron needles. Sailors would place the magnetized needle on a chip of wood so it would float on water. It always pointed north-south, and thus could be used to guide their ships.

Overview: *Students will make a simple compass.*

Materials

- circular magnets (one per student)
- steel straight pins (one per student)
- small chips of a Styrofoam cup
- aluminum pie plates partially filled with water
- transparency of page 16

- pinch of iron filings on small pieces of paper
- overhead projector
- bar magnet suspended from the ceiling
- *optional*: compass (available from Delta Education or nature stores)
- lined paper, pencils, rulers, crayons

Activity

1. Tell students that nonmagnetized material which is attracted to a magnet can be temporarily magnetized, using a magnet. Show the students that the straight pin you are about to magnetize is not a magnet by dipping it into a pinch of iron filings on an overhead projector. (*If it is not magnetized, the iron filings should not stick to it. A few particles of the filings may adhere even to a nonmagnetized pin, but more will do so after it is magnetized.*)

2. Demonstrate how the pin can be magnetized by pressing one straight pin against the projector glass, holding it firmly at the head end. Using the flat side of a circular magnet, stroke the pin from the head end to the point, lifting the magnet when you reach the point of the pin. Return to the head of the pin and stroke it again, pushing the magnet firmly against the pin as you do so. Continue stroking the magnet firmly and quickly *in one direction only*, counting about 50 strokes.

3. Show the students that the pin is now magnetized by dipping it into the iron filings again. It should pick up a cluster of the iron filings.

4. Use page 16 to review the process by which the pie was magnetized. Distribute a pin and magnet to each student and have them magnetize their pins in the same manner as you demonstrated.

5. Give each group a pinch of iron filings on a paper so they can test their pins' magnetism by dipping them into the iron filings. If not many filings stick, have them continue stroking their pins with the magnet for about 25 strokes.

6. Let them test their pins to see if they repel or attract another magnetized pin. This can be done by laying a magnetized pin on the table and touching the point or head of another magnetized pin to the point or head of the pin on the table. (*The first pin should attract or repel the other pin, depending upon the location of the poles of each pin. Some pins may have north at the head of the pin, while others may have north at the pointed end. This is determined by the side of the magnet being used during the magnetizing process.*)

14   © Teacher Created Resources, Inc.

Making a Compass (cont.)

Activity (cont.)

7. Have students reverse *one* of the pins and repeat the experiment; if they repelled before, they should now attract and vice versa.

8. Distribute a chip of Styrofoam to each student and help them gently push their pins through it so the head and point of each pin are exposed and the pin is parallel to the surfaces of the Styrofoam. This becomes the compass needle.

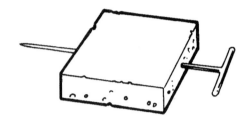

9. Provide each group with a pie pan of water. Have students place one compass needle in the center of the pan of water and watch how it moves. After it has come to rest, compare it with the bar magnet hanging from the ceiling. The pin should be pointing in the same direction.

10. Have the students gently push each compass needle around; it should return to the same direction. If it floats to the side of the pan, gently return it to the center. If it does not line up north-south, the magnetism is weak and the pin needs to be rubbed head-to-point another 50 strokes. Let students test their compass needles one at a time in the pan of water. (If two or more pins are placed in the pan at the same time, they will attract to each other rather than to Earth's magnetic field.)

Closure

- Show the students an actual compass, if available, and have them compare the direction its needle is pointing with the direction of the bar magnet hanging from the ceiling and the direction of the floating compass needles.

- Show them the magnetite which was used in the first activity in this series and show that it is a natural magnet by dipping it into iron filings. Explain that magnetite was used by early sailors to create magnetic needles and simple compasses much as the students have done.

- Distribute lined paper, pencils, rulers, crayons, and drawing paper to each student. Tell students to imagine they have suddenly become magnetic. Have them write about how this would change their lives. Tell them to make drawings to go along with their stories and label the parts of their drawing.

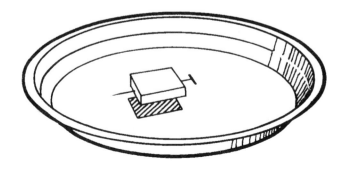

Making a Compass *(cont.)*

Making a Magnet

In an ordinary pin, the atoms are not arranged in any particular order. As you run the magnet over the pin, the atoms line up with the positive end pointing one way and the negative the other. Stroking the pin many times strengthens this alignment.

The pin is only a temporary magnet, however, and the magnetism gets weaker with time. If the pin is hit hard with a hammer or is heated, it will lose its magnetism.

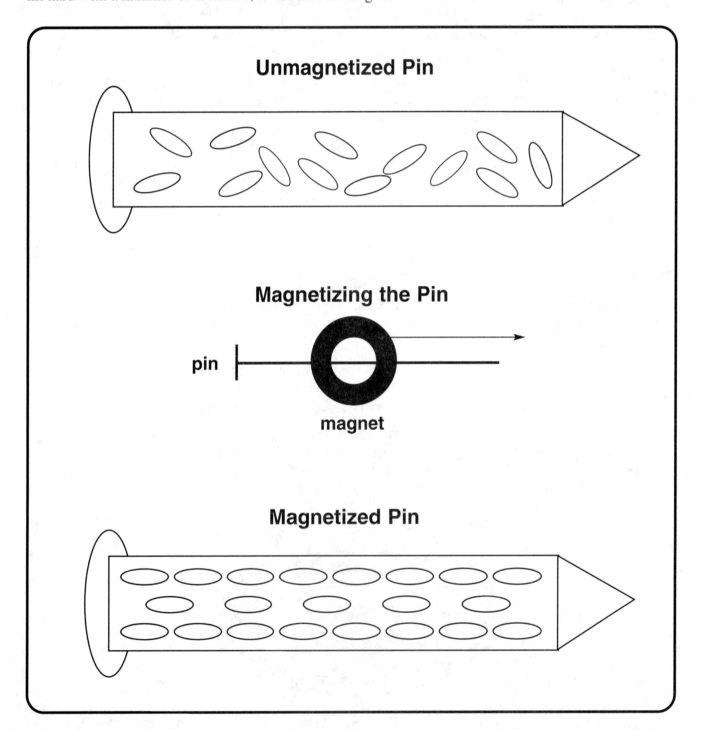

Static Cling

Teacher Information

Electricity is sometimes classified as *static electricity* and *current electricity*. Both are made up of the same kind of particles. Static electricity consists of electrons or ions that do not move. Current electricity is made up of moving electrons or ions. Almost all the electricity we use is current electricity.

An object becomes electrically charged if it gains or loses electrons. For example, if a glass rod is rubbed with a piece of silk cloth, the rod loses electrons and becomes positively charged. You can create static electricity by running an inflated balloon over your hair briskly on a dry day. Your hair loses electrons and becomes positively charged. The balloon gains electrons and becomes negatively charged. The static electricity may make your hair crackle as you rub it with the balloon.

Static electricity can be investigated using a variety of materials which can be given a static charge. This is most effective during dry weather, or in a room which is being heated or air conditioned and, therefore, has less moisture in the air.

Overview: *Students will investigate static electricity.*

Materials

- balloons
- string
- parent letter (page 18)

Activity

1. Ask the students if they have ever been shocked after walking across a rug on a dry day. Explain that this is called *static electricity*. Tell the students that they are going to investigate this type of electricity.

2. Give each student an inflated balloon tied to a string (or let them inflate their own). Demonstrate how to build a static charge by vigorously rubbing the balloon over your hair. As you pull the balloon away, some of the hair will begin to stand upright. Have the students try this with their own hair.

3. Have them rub the balloon against their hair again. Tell them to see if they can stick the balloon on the wall. (*If they have created an electrical charge, it should. If not, have them rub the balloon again.*)

4. After charging the balloon against their hair, let them hold it by the string and bring it near another student's balloon. (*The balloons may pull together or push apart.*)

Closure

- With each child, send home a deflated balloon and the letter on the next page so students can continue to investigate static electricity at home.

Static Cling *(cont.)*

Parent Letter

Date_____

Dear Parents,

Your child has had fun investigating static electricity by using an inflated balloon today at school. Please help him or her to inflate a balloon and tie it to a string. Let him or her show you what the class has been doing with the balloon in the classroom.

The students have been told to try finding what they can rub against their balloons at home to see if they can get them to stick to a wall or their clothing. You may want to help your child find a variety of things to use to build a static charge, such as the carpet, upholstery, drapes, or a pet's fur.

On the lines below, your child should write about what he or she discovered with the balloon and then draw a picture of the experiment. Please have your child bring this paper back to class to share with us tomorrow.

Sincerely,

_____

_____

_____

_____

_____

_____

_____

Make a drawing of your balloon experiment here.

The Magic of Static

Teacher Information

Static electricity can be investigated using a variety of materials which can be given a static charge. This is most effective during dry weather or in a room which is being heated or air conditioned and, therefore, has less moisture in the air.

Overview: *Students will have fun investigating the magic of static electricity.*

Materials

- balloons
- small wool duster or piece of wool cloth
- 8" x 10" (20 cm x 25 cm) clear plastic boxes used for pictures (available where picture frames are sold)
- paper circles from a hole punch (*optional:* confetti)
- Styrofoam packing peanuts or pieces
- bottles of water
- buckets or basins
- data sheets and instructions for each workstation (pages 22–25)
- transparency of page 20

Lesson Preparation

- Set up stations for students to rotate through using the information on the data sheets. If possible, set up duplicates of each station to have fewer students at each of them.
- Test each of the stations and adjust the setup as needed to match the students' ability levels.
- Establish a rotation system which will allow at least 15 minutes at each station.
- Arrange for adult or older student volunteers to be assigned to each station to assist the students as needed, if they are not able to do the work alone.

Activity

1. Introduce the students to each of the stations. Explain the instructions which they are to follow as they work at each of them. Demonstrate how they are to use the materials at the various stations.
2. Divide the students into groups of three or four students and assign each group to begin at a different station. Allow sufficient time for each group to explore the materials at their station before moving them on to the next. This lesson should be spread over more than one day to enable the students to benefit from experimenting with the materials and sharing their ideas.

Closure

- When all students have visited each of the stations, have each group demonstrate one of the exciting new discoveries they made as they investigated static electricity.
- Invite another group of students to visit the classroom and have your students show them the discoveries they made about static electricity.
- Use the transparency (page 20) to review the lesson.

The Magic of Static *(cont.)*

Particles and Electric Fields

Normally, an atom has an equal number of electrons and protons, and so it is electrically neutral. If an atom gains some electrons, it becomes negatively charged. If an atom loses some electrons, it becomes positively charged. Atoms that have an electric charge—either positive or negative—are called *ions*.

Every particle is surrounded by an *electric field*. Charged particles exert a force on one another, even when not touching, because each electric field extends into the space around each particle.

Uncharged Particles

If two balloons are uncharged, they do not exert any force between them.

Particles with Unlike Charges

If one balloon is charged positively and the other negatively, their electric fields interact and pull them together.

Particles with Like Charges

If two balloons are each negatively (or each positively) charged, their electric fields interact and cause them to move apart.

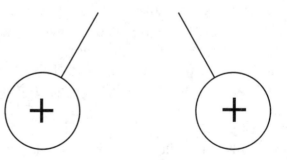

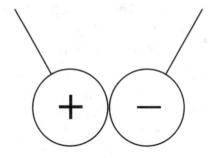

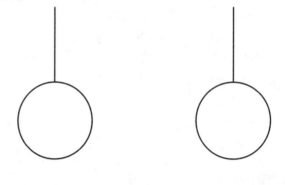

The Magic of Static *(cont.)*

Answer Key

Station 1

Popping Paper

Some of the circles jump from the paper to the plastic box. Others jump back and forth, while still others remain on the paper but stand on edge. There is a popping sound made as the circles hit the plastic box. If left alone for a while, the circles lose the static charge but can be reactivated by rubbing the box again.

Station 2

Jumping Peanuts

If the charged balloon is held about three inches (7.5 cm) above the Styrofoam peanuts, they will leap up and cling to it. When shaken gently, the peanuts continue to adhere to the balloon. They can be chased around the balloon when another charged peanut on the balloon is pushed toward them.

Station 3

Weird Water

The stream of water will bend away from the charged balloon when it is held about one inch (2.5 cm) from it.

Station 4

Dancing Balloons

When both hanging balloons are charged with the duster, they will repel each other. If a hand is placed between the balloons, they will be attracted to the hand but will move away (repelling) from each other when the hand is removed.

The Magic of Static (cont.)

Station 1: Popping Paper

Materials

- clear plastic box
- about 40 paper circles from a hole punch

Setup

- Put the paper circles on the table top and put the clear plastic box over them.

How to Do the Test

1. Have one person hold the plastic box down over the paper circles.

2. Rub the top of the plastic box with your hand as fast as you can.

Watch to See What Happens

1. Do any circles begin to jump?_____

2. Are there any circles standing on edge?_____

3. Do any circles leap up and hang from the box?_____

4. Are there any sounds being made?_____

5. If you heard sounds, what did they sound like?_____

Try something new and then make a picture of what you discovered.

The Magic of Static *(cont.)*

Station 2: Jumping Peanuts

Materials

- inflated balloon

- handful of Styrofoam packing peanuts

- wool duster or wool cloth

Setup

- Put a balloon, wool duster or cloth,
  and Styrofoam packing peanuts on the table.

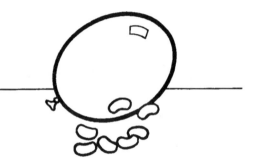

How to Do the Test

1. Rub the balloon with the wool duster.

2. Hold the balloon near the peanuts.

Watch to See What Happens

1. Do the peanuts jump on the balloon?_____

2. Shake the balloon gently. Do the peanuts stick to it?_____

3. What happens if you pull or push the peanuts around on the balloon?

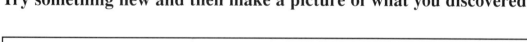

Try something new and then make a picture of what you discovered.

The Magic of Static *(cont.)*

Station 3: Weird Water

Materials

- inflated balloon
- wool duster or wool cloth
- bottle of water
- bucket or basin
- towels

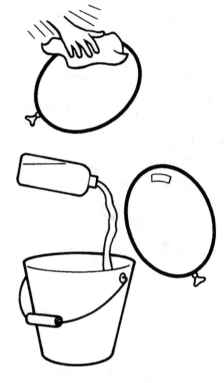

Setup

- Put all the materials on the table.

How to Do the Test

1. Rub the balloon with the wool duster.

2. Pour the water slowly into the bucket. Hold the balloon near the water.

Watch to See What Happens

1. Did the water run straight down from the bottle?_____

2. Do this same test two more times and see what happens. Be sure to refill the bottle and to rub the balloon with the duster each time. Tell what happens each time.

_____

Try something new and then make a picture of what you discovered.

The Magic of Static *(cont.)*

Station 4: Dancing Balloons

Materials

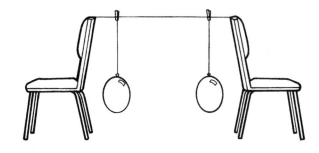

- 2 inflated balloons of different colors, each on a string
- wool duster or wool cloth
- 3 feet (90 cm) string
- 2 clamp-on clothespins
- 2 chairs

Setup

- Place the chairs close together and stretch the string taut between them. Put the clothespins on it two feet (60 cm) apart. Hang the balloons from the clothespins so they are level with each other.

How to Do the Test

1. Rub one balloon with the wool duster.

Watch to See What Happens

1. What happens after only one balloon was rubbed with the duster?

   _____

2. What happens if both balloons are rubbed?

   _____

3. What happens when you put your hand between the balloons?

   _____

Try something new and then make a picture of what you discovered.

The Electron Dance

Overview: *Students will do a dance to simulate the action of electrons within an atom.*

Materials

- 2 basketballs labeled "neutron" (+/–)
- 2 volleyballs labeled "proton" (+)
- 2 Ping-Pong balls labeled "electron" (–)
- transparency of Parts of an Atom (page 28)
- 4 index cards to be used as labels on large balls
- 2 8 1/2" x 11" (22 cm x 28 cm) pieces of card stock labeled "Nucleus" and "The Atom"
- 9 feet (2.7 m) of string with chalk tied on one end and a loop on the other

Lesson Preparation

- Select a helper to make the outlines on a large paved area (e.g., playground) for the electron dance. Use the chalk on the end of the strung to draw one circle on the paved area to represent the nucleus. The helper should stand in the middle and hold the loop end of the string while the end with the chalk is stretched to draw a circle of a two-foot (61 cm) radius. Draw two larger circles with their centers in the middle of the nucleus circle. The circles should have radii of six and nine feet respectively (1.8 m and 2.7 m). These are orbits of the electrons.

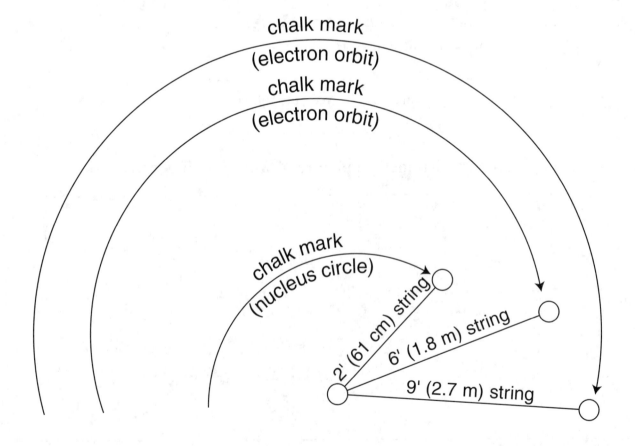

The Electron Dance (cont.)

Activity

1. Use the transparency of Parts of an Atom (page 28) to explain how an atom works. Explain how the students are to move outside to simulate an atom, including the motion of the electrons around the nucleus. Go to the area used for the simulation.

2. Select students to be electrons (2); neutrons (2), protons (2), and give each the appropriately labeled balls to hold.

3. Select two students to hold the large signs "Nucleus" and "The Atom."

4. Station the protons and neutrons inside the center of circle. Have the sign "Nucleus" held inside this circle also.

5. Place the two electrons on their orbit.

6. Place the person with "The Atom" sign outside the circles.

7. Remind students that the nucleus consists of protons and neutrons, represented by larger balls since nearly all the mass of the atom is in its nucleus. Point out that the electrons have much less mass than the protons and neutrons.

8. Tell the "players" that on your signal, the electrons should begin running around the nucleus, staying on the circle (orbit). Stop the students after they have raced around the nucleus several times.

Closure

- Review the fact that although they were moving fast, and on the same plane (the pavement), real electrons travel so fast and all around the nucleus that they would appear to be a sphere, much like a bubble.

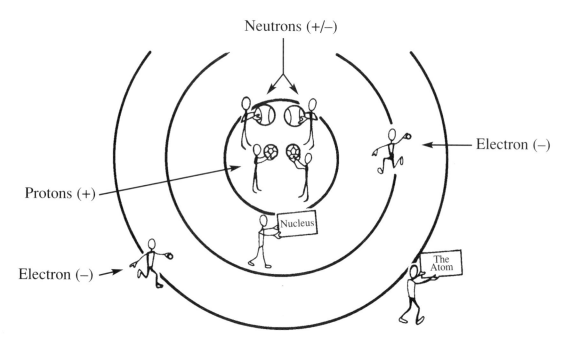

The Electron Dance *(cont.)*

Parts of an Atom

Matter has mass and takes up space. Atoms are basic building blocks of matter. Atoms are made up of three types of particles: *protons, neutrons,* and *electrons*. Protons and neutrons make up most of the mass of the atom. In a 150-pound person, for example, 149 pounds and 15 ounces are protons and neutrons while only one ounce is electrons. The mass of an electron is very small.

The nucleus of the atom has both the protons and neutrons. Protons have a positive (+) charge, and neutrons have no (+/−) charge—they are neutral. Electrons orbit around the nucleus. They have a negative (−) charge. The electron orbits are spherical around the nucleus, not a flat plane like the orbits of the planets around the sun. The electrons move so fast that they form a shell around the nucleus, much like the blades of a fan, which prevents anything passing through them as they spin.

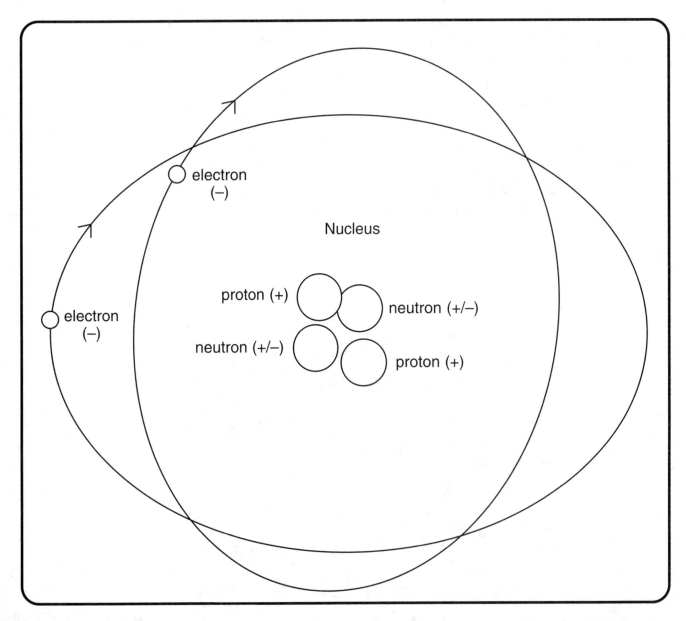

Light Bulbs and Batteries

Can You Light the Light Bulb?

Overview: *Students will each light a flashlight bulb (2.5 volt) using only a wire and D cell battery.*

Materials (Note: See page 48 for suppliers of materials needed for the electricity activities.)
- D cell battery
- flashlight bulb (2.5 volt)
- 6" (15 cm) length of insulated wire with both ends stripped of insulation (Use telephone wire purchased at an electronics supply store.)
- wire strippers

Activity

1. Ask students if they have ever used a flashlight. Have them draw how they think it works. Save their drawings for later, when they do the activity of constructing a flashlight.

2. Distribute one bulb, wire, and battery to each student. Instruct them to make the light bulb work using only these three pieces of equipment.

3. Do not assist the students in any way. One student will eventually find a way of attaching the equipment and the bulb will light. After a few more students are successful, have the first student who did light his or her bulb go to the board and draw exactly how he or she did this. Draw the battery for the students so that it is large enough for all students to see and then, have the student add a large bulb and the wire to show exactly where the connections are needed to light the bulb.

4. Tell the students there are four ways to connect the equipment to light the bulb (see below), but do not tell them how this is done. Let them continue working until they discover them. When additional ways are discovered, have them drawn on the board.

Closure

- Have the students draw the four different methods for connecting the wire, battery, and bulb to make the light work.

Light Bulbs and Batteries *(cont.)*

How Does a Light Bulb Work?

Overview: *Students learn what how a light bulb works.*

Materials (Each student will need the following materials.)

- same items as used in the previous lesson
- magnifiers
- 2 index cards
- 6 inches (15 cm) yarn
- Optional: burned out 2.5 volt bulbs and regular clear light bulbs
- transparency of the light bulb information (page 31)

Lesson Preparation

- Carefully remove the metal casing from a 2.5 volt bulb, using wire strippers or other tools. Wear gloves while doing this work. Try to expose the area in the base to show where the location of the wires which support the filament inside the bulb. (See diagram of bulb.) If possible, preserve the connections of these wires with the base so student will see where they are attached.

Activity

1. Have the students draw a picture of the light bulb on the index card, large enough to fill it half way, saving room to draw the battery below it later. Tell them to use their magnifiers to see the details and include them in their drawings. It is especially important that they show where the wires are connected to the base and the location and shape of the filament. Show them the bulbs you have prepared for them so they can see where these wires connect.

2. Discuss what the students have drawn and then show them the transparency and explain the parts of the bulb. Have them compare these with their drawings. If they did not draw where the wires connected to the base, have them do so now.

Closure

- Have the students light their bulb with the battery using one wire. Tell them to look at the position they need to place the wire and battery in order to get it to light. Have them try all four positions so they can see that the base and side of the bulb need to be contacted for the bulb to work.

- Tell them to look at the filament to see how it reacts when the bulb lights. (It get red hot and glows.)

- Have the students draw the battery below their bulb on the index card. Give them a piece of yarn to be glued in place to show where it must be located in order to light the bulb.

Light Bulbs and Batteries *(cont.)*

Parts of a Light Bulb

100–watt bulb

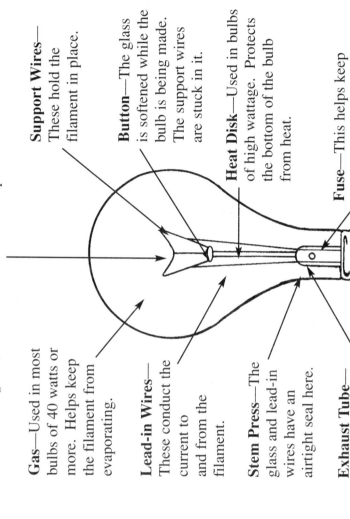

Filament—The wire that heats up to *incandescence* (in-can-des-cents), or glowing, white heat. When Thomas Edison used a cotton sewing thread as his first filament, it burned to an ash. Today, the filament is made of *tungsten*, which does not melt except under extreme heat.

Gas—Used in most bulbs of 40 watts or more. Helps keep the filament from evaporating.

Lead-in Wires—These conduct the current to and from the filament.

Stem Press—The glass and lead-in wires have an airtight seal here.

Exhaust Tube—Through this tube, air is taken out of the bulb and the gas is pumped in. The tube is sealed off so the base will fit over it.

Support Wires—These hold the filament in place.

Button—The glass is softened while the bulb is being made. The support wires are stuck in it.

Heat Disk—Used in bulbs of high wattage. Protects the bottom of the bulb from heat.

Fuse—This helps keep the bulb from cracking and prevents blowing of electric fuses.

Base

2.5–volt bulb

coiled wire (filament)

bead to separate wires

straight wires (2), one leading to solder point on bottom, the other leading to solder on the edge of the metal base

solder

Completing the Circuit

1. Current passes from the negative end of the battery through wire soldered to the side of the metal casing on the light bulb.

2. Current continues through this wire to the support wire attached to one side of the filament, across the filament, and back into the other support wire which is attached to the bottom of the bulb.

3. Current passes back into the positive end of the battery and then to the negative end where it flows into the wire again.

Light Bulbs and Batteries *(cont.)*

Dissecting a Battery

Overview: *Students will examine a dissected battery to see its parts and learn how they work.*

Materials

- D cell battery
- plastic wrap
- hacksaw, needle nosed pliers, gloves, vise
- copies of page 34 (one per student)
- transparency of the diagram of the Cross Section of a Dry Cell Battery (page 33)

Lesson Preparation

- Use the hacksaw to cut a D battery in half lengthwise by placing it in a vise. Wear gloves while doing this task. After the battery is cut in half, cover it with plastic wrap.

Activity

1. Divide the students into small groups and give each group a battery and paper. Have them discuss and then draw what they think it looks like inside.

2. Have the groups share their pictures and describe them.

Closure

- Show the picture of the Dry Cell Battery (page 33) and discuss the parts of the battery.

- Show the battery which has been cut in half and let the students compare it to the diagram on the transparency.

- Give each student a battery, wire, and a light bulb and have them light it four different ways. Ask them to look at the diagram and cut battery to imagine what is happening inside the battery.

- Test to see if the battery will light the bulb by placing the wire and light bulb in positions used before to light the bulb. Unless the battery is dead, the bulb should light.

- Have the students once again draw what the inside of a battery looks like and then add a bulb to one end. They should draw a line to show how the circuit is completed to make the bulb light up.

- Have the students complete the work sheet "Will the Bulb Light?". After completing this, let them check their work using a battery, light bulb, and wire. (*The bulbs that will not work are numbers 1, 3, 6, and 7. Number 5 can only work when the bases of all three bulbs touch each other, the end of the wire touches one of the bulb's metal base, and one of the bulb's bottom makes contact with the battery.*)

Light Bulbs and Batteries *(cont.)*

Cross Section of a Dry Cell Battery

A dry cell battery consists of a zinc container with chemicals inside it that produce an electric current by reacting with one another. The battery has a positive (+) and a negative (–) terminal. The container is the negative terminal, a carbon rod in the center serves as the positive terminal. Energy is sent from one terminal and through an object, such as a light bulb, and back to the other terminal to complete the circuit. Electrical current then flows from the battery and through the bulb to make it light.

Dry Cell Battery

Top cover

Asphalt seal

Carbon rod

Separator

Zinc container

Positive terminal

Air space

Manganese dioxide

Paper or metal jacket

Bottom cover and negative terminal

Light Bulbs and Batteries *(cont.)*

Will the Bulb Light?

To the Student: Look at the drawings below and decide which ones show connections that will light the bulb. Circle **Y** on the battery if the bulb will light. If you think it will not work, circle **N**.

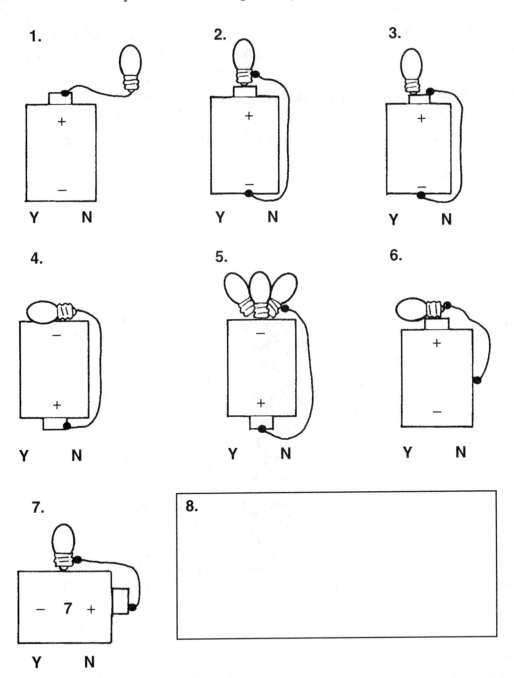

1.

Y   N

2.

Y   N

3.

Y   N

4.

Y   N

5.

Y   N

6.

Y   N

7.

Y   N

8.

- Use the equipment you need to test each of the seven methods and check your answers.

- Draw the changes needed in the pictures you marked N to show how to make the bulb light.

- In the box, draw another way to connect the battery, bulb, and wire to make the bulb light

Light Bulbs and Batteries *(cont.)*

Building a Flashlight

Overview: *Students will construct a flashlight with simple materials.*

Materials

- same materials as used in Can You Light the Light Bulb? (Use a 12"/30cm length of insulated wire.)
- masking tape
- cardboard tubes (toilet paper rolls work well)
- aluminum foil
- drawings of a flashlight made by the students in the first lesson of this series
- a flashlight

Lesson Preparation

- Construct a flashlight from a bulb, two batteries, and one long wire. Use the cardboard tube to hold the batteries. Use tape to hold the bulb on to the battery so that it will make contact. Coil the wire around the base of the bulb so it will light. Foil may be used as a reflector around the light and as a switch. The drawing below shows one way to make a flashlight. There are other combinations of the equipment which will also work.

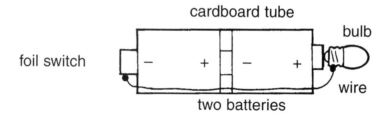

Activity

1. Divide the students into groups and give each of them a bulb, long wire, and two batteries. Have them connect their batteries, wire and bulb so it will light.

2. Distribute a cardboard tube, pieces of foil, and 6 inches (12 cm) of tape to each group. Explain that they are to build a flashlight that can be turned on and off. Tell them they may have more tape or foil if needed but not additional wires, batteries, or bulbs.

Closure

- Have each group explain how they constructed their flashlight.

- Darken the room and let each group demonstrate how their flashlight works. Compare the various models for brightness and ability for shining the light the greatest distance.

- Show the parts of a real flashlight to the students and let the students make a drawing of how they think it works.

- Have the students compare their new drawings with those made at the beginning of this study.

Electric Circuits

Constructing an Electric Circuit

Overview: *Students will construct simple electric circuits.*

Materials (Each student will need the following.)

- 2 (6"/15cm) lengths of insulated, stripped at ends
- flashlight bulb (2.5 volt)
- light bulb socket
- battery
- battery holder

(Note: See page 48 to locate equipment battery and battery holder suppliers.)

Lesson Preparation

- Order the bulb sockets and battery holders in time to be used for this lesson.
- Experiment with constructing a circuit in order to experience some of the problems which students may encounter during this activity.

Activity

1. Distribute the materials to the students and tell them they are to experiment with assembling them to light the bulb.

2. Show them how to use the connectors on the sockets to hold the wires, as shown below. Do not show them how to assemble the circuit as they will discover this for themselves.

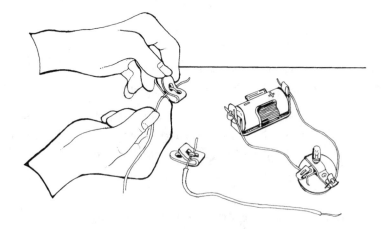

Closure

- Have the students discuss how the electricity was transferred in the "Can You Light the Light Bulb?" experiment. Ask them to compare this with the setup they have just constructed using the socket and battery holder. Tell them to trace how the electricity flows from the battery, to the bulb, and back into the battery.

Electric Circuits (cont.)

How Does a Circuit Work?

Overview: *Students will discover series and parallel electric circuits.*

Materials

- battery, battery holder, socket, bulb, 2 wires for each student
- copies of Constructing Circuits activity sheet (page 38)

Lesson Preparation

- Follow the instructions on the Constructing Circuits work sheet to build the circuits and then do the experiments. You will find when one of the bulbs in the parallel circuit is loosened in its socket, the other lights continue to light. The electricity can continue to flow through the next wire. When this is repeated with the series circuit, none of the bulbs will light. The series circuit has only a single wire linking the bulbs. When the bulb is loosened, electricity cannot flow through the bulb and, thus, the circuit is broken.

Activity

1. Divide the students into groups of three or four and distribute materials to each student. Let each student construct a circuit.

2. Let students experiment with the equipment, linking up bulbs, batteries, and sockets in various ways. Tell them they should never link more than two batteries to a single bulb or it will send too much electricity through it and burn it out. (Note: Should this happen, have the students examine the bulb with a magnifier to discover why it no longer lights. The filament becomes so overheated that it melts at one point and breaks. This stops the flow of electricity through the bulb.)

3. Distribute page 38. Have students construct the parallel and series circuits as shown, and then answer the questions.

Answers

1. When bulb 1 is unscrewed, the other lights remain illuminated.

2. When any of the bulbs is unscrewed, the others remain illuminated.

3. The electricity flows from the battery, to the socket, through the bulb, and back to the battery. Electricity flows in this same way for each of the sockets.

4. When bulb A is unscrewed, the other two lights go out also.

5. When any of the bulbs are unscrewed, all other lights go out.

6. The electricity flows from the battery to the first socket, through the bulb, and directly on to the next sockets and bulbs, returns to the battery, and continues the flow.

7. When one ligh goes out in a parallel circuit, the others remain illuminated. When one light goes out in a series circuit, none of the other lights are illuminated.

8. The electricity in a parallel circuit will bypass the bulb which is not illuminated and still light up the other bulbs. This cannot happen in a series circuit since the link is broken when any one of the bulbs burns out and electricity cannot flow to the next one and back to the battery.

Closure

- Discuss the answers to page 38 with the students.

Extender

- Have the students work in small groups and use two batteries and three sockets to reconstruct the circuits on the work sheet. Let them compare the difference made by the extra battery. *(The lights will burn more brightly since 1.5 volts is being added.)*

Electric Circuits (cont.)

Constructing Circuits

To the Students: Parallel circuits are constructed with two wires running side by side. Series circuits have a continuous circle of wire. Construct each of these circuits as shown below. Answer the questions about each of these as you finish building it. (Answer questions 1–6 on the back of this page. Complete numbers 7 and 8 on the lines provided.

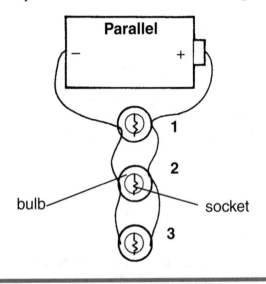

1. Unscrew the bulb in socket 1 just until it goes out. What happens to the bulbs in the other sockets?

2. Tighten the bulb again and then repeat this experiment by unscrewing each of the other bulbs, one bulb at a time. Did the other bulbs go out?

3. Use a colored pencil and trace the electricity from the battery to bulbs 1, 2, and 3 and then back to the battery.

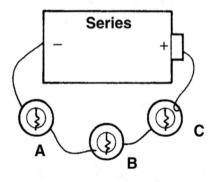

4. Unscrew the bulb in socket A. What happened to the other bulbs?

5. Repeat this by unscrewing each of the other bulbs, one bulb at a time. What happened to the bulbs?

6. Use a colored pencil and trace the electricity from the battery to bulbs A, B, and C.

7. Compare the parallel and series circuits. Tell what was different about them when you unscrewed the bulbs. _____

_____

8. Explain why they were different. _____

_____

_____

_____

_____

Electric Circuits *(cont.)*

Inventing Circuits

Overview: *Students will apply what they have learned about circuits and develop combinations of them to increase their understanding of how they work.*

Materials

- copies of page 40 (one per student)

  Each group will need the following items:
- 2 batteries
- 8 wires
- 4 sockets
- 4 bulbs
- 2 battery holders

Activity

1. Distribute a copy of page 40 to each student. Have them predict which of the circuits will or will not work.

2. Divide the students into small groups and distribute the equipment needed to test each of the circuits. Let them construct each of the circuits and then check their original answers.

Closure

- Discuss the answers with the students. *(Circuits B, C, and D will work. Circuit A does not work since the electricity will flow through the batteries but not the bulb. This is called a short circuit, in which the electric energy seeks the shortest path. If one of the batteries in A is turned around, the bulb will light. It is not as bright as when two batteries are connected end to end. When the batteries are connected + to + and – to – and then through the bulb, the electricity flows from one battery to the other and into the bulb rather than combining the electricity of both batteries as shown in D.)*

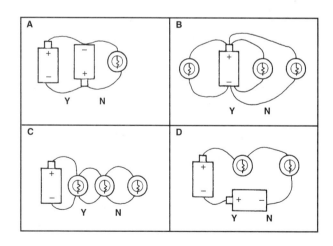

Electric Circuits *(cont.)*

Will the Circuit Work?

To the Students: Look at the circuits below carefully to decide if you think the light bulbs will light up or not.

1. Circle **Y** if you think the circuit will work or **N** if you think it will not work.

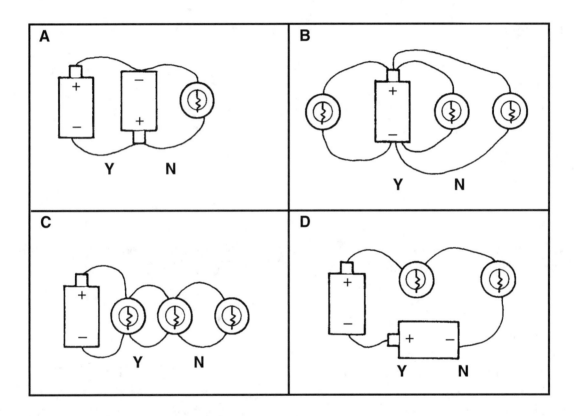

2. Construct each circuit and check your answers.

3. Write the letter(s) of those circuit(s) where your prediction was wrong._____

4. Which circuit did not work? _____Why?_____

_____

Work with the batteries and light bulb to make the circuit work. Describe what you had to do to get the circuit to work._____

_____

_____

Electric Circuits (cont.)

Searching for Conductors

Overview: *Students will test a variety of objects to find what will conduct electricity.*

Materials Each group will need the following items:

- battery
- variety of materials to check as conductors, including metal and non-metal items such as these: yarn, coin, pipe cleaner, paper, cardboard, marble, foil, paper clip, and pencil with lead exposed (Pencil lead is graphite which will conduct electricity.)
- battery holder
- 3 wires
- bulb
- socket
- small baggies

Lesson Preparation

- Assemble materials which students will use to check as conductors. Make identical sets of these to place in baggies for each group to use.

Activity

1. Divide the students into small groups and give each a baggie of materials. Have them sort these into piles, separating those through which they think electricity will pass and those which will not conduct it.
2. When this is finished, write **Yes** and **No** on the board. List the results of each group's sorting beneath the two categories. Some of the items will appear in both categories.
3. Distribute the electrical equipment to each group and have them construct a tester (see diagram below).
4. Demonstrate how to touch the wires leading from the battery and the socket to the item being tested. Explain that if the item is a conductor, electricity will flow through it and the bulb will light up. Be sure the students test the tester's connections first by touching the two wires together to see if the bulb lights. Have them test each item and sort them again.

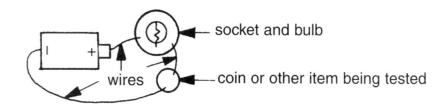

Closure

- Discuss what the students discovered. (Electricity will flow through all the metal items.)
- Have the students do this test on other items in the classroom to find which are conductors.
- Demonstrate that electricity will also flow through water by holding the wires close together in a glass of water. You may need to use two batteries to provide more energy to the bulbs.

Mystery Connections

Overview: *Students will discover how electricity flows through various connections of wires.*

Materials

- 8 shoebox lids
- various lengths of 1/2-inch (1.3 cm) wide foil strips (or use insulated wire)
- 64 brass fasteners
- 8 pieces of card stock
- conductor testers (See page 41.)
- Mystery Connections Record (page 44)
- masking tape

Lesson Preparation

- Label the eight box lids A–H and then number them on top of the lids as shown in the diagrams below.

- Punch holes near the numbers and insert brass fasteners through them, keeping the heads of the brass fasteners on the outside of the lid. Make sure the holes are no farther apart than the longer strip of foil or wire.

- Attach wires or thin strips of foil to the brass fasteners on the undersides of the lids. Be sure the contact is firm by bending the prongs of the brass fasteners over the foil or wrapping the tip of the wire around them before bending the prongs. If foil is used, place masking tape over each strip, including the prongs of the brass fasteners, to prevent the foil strips from making contact with each other.

- Write the numbers near the prongs inside the lids to correspond with those on the outside.

- Test the boxes and make a record for each of them to serve as answers.

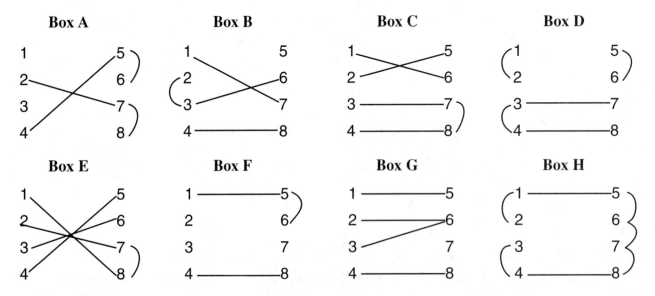

- Fit card stock inside the box lids to hide the wires. This will be removed for students to check their work so it should not be permanently taped into the lids.

Electric Circuits (cont.)

Mystery Connections (cont.)

Activity

1. Divide the students in eight groups and distribute the materials for them to construct a tester. Provide them with a box lid and copy of Mystery Connections Record (page 44).

2. Read the instructions with the students and have each group test their connections between #1 and #2 brass fasteners. As they work, monitor their progress.

3. When all brass fasteners have been tested, students may remove the card stock cover and compare the locations of the wires with the drawings they made on their record sheet.

4. When a group finishes their box, they should place it on a table and take another one to continue testing them. It is not necessary to complete all boxes.

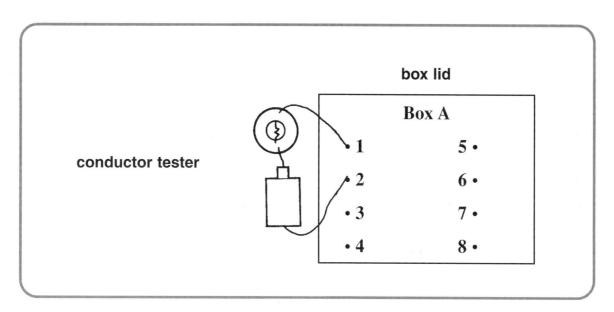

Closure

• Have the students discuss what they discovered when comparing the location of the wires with the connections the tester detected and they recorded. Ask them to explain how the light could go on without having a wire directly connected to that brass fastener. (Electricity will flow via another connection as shown in the diagram below.)

| 1   5 ⟩ | The light in the tester will work when brads 2 and 5 are touched because electricity will be able to flow from 2–6–5 to close the circuit. |
| 2 ——————— 6 ⟩ | |

Electric Circuits (cont.)

Mystery Connections Record

To the Students: Use the conductor tester to find the connections between the brass fasteners in the shoebox lid. Follow the instructions below to see how to do the test.

1. Write the letter of your box on the record below in both the columns.

2. Press the tip of one wire of the tester to brad #1 and press the other wire to brad #2.

3. If the light goes on, draw a line between #1 and #2 on the record in the "Connections" column. Do not draw a line if the light does not go on.

4. Continue to press one wire to #1 brad and move the other wire to the #3 brad. Again, draw a line on the record if the light goes on.

5. Repeat this process, always holding the wire on #1 brad until you have checked the brads 2–8 and recorded the results.

6. Next, move the wire to brad #2 and test all the others to find the connections, recording those which light the bulb.

Connections Box _____		Wires Box _____	
1	5	1	5
2	6	2	6
3	7	3	7
4	8	4	8

7. After all the brads have been tested for connections, remove the cover inside the box and look at where the wires are. Draw these wires on the record in the "Wires" column.

8. Compare the location of the wires and the connections you recorded. Sometimes a brad did not have a direct wire connected to another brad but the light went on when you tested them. Draw and explain how the electricity could flow between these unconnected brads.

9. Exchange boxes with another group and test to find the connections. Record these below.

Connections Box _____		Wires Box _____	
1	5	1	5
2	6	2	6
3	7	3	7
4	8	4	8

Electricity Assessment

To the Teacher: This is a performance-based assessment which will enable students to demonstrate what they have learned from this study. There will be four tasks for students to perform independently. The activities, materials, and answers are described on the chart.

Task	Activity	Materials	Answers
1	lighting a bulb in four different ways	• 1 bulb • 1 D-cell battery • 1 long insulated wire	
2	test for conductors	• bulb, battery, socket, 3 wires • items used in activity: Searching for Conductors (page 41)	• list of items with metal in them and pencil lead (graphite) • sentence stating that only metal conducts electricity
3	identifying circuits	• Box C, used in Mystery Connections (page 42)	• connections: 1–6; 5–2; 3–7; 7–8; 4–8; 3–4; 4–7; 8–3 • electricity travels between 3 and 4 via a route through 3–7–8–4.
4	predicting circuits	• answer sheet (Task 4, page 47)	• NO: #1 (needs another wire); #4 (connect wire to socket); #5 (add bulb)

Administering the Assessment

• Gather the materials needed for each of the tasks. This assessment can be done by the entire class at one time by providing enough stations for each student to work independently. Divide the work areas with cardboard barriers to provide privacy. Work out a rotation system for students to move from task to task on a given signal. The diagram above shows one possible method to do this. Each station has the materials for that task, except #4 which requires only the answer sheet. Label each station with the task number.

• Students should be given a set time to complete the task and then all rotate at the same time. Adjust the time to the ability levels of the students.

• During the assessment, students should not be permitted to talk.

• Monitor the students' progress and be prepared to substitute equipment and pencils as needed.

Instructions to be Read to the Students

• Review the tasks students will perform during the assessment and explain the rotation system.

• Tell the students you will announce when there are five and then two minutes remaining for them to work on the task.

• Let students know that there is to be no talking or looking at another student's work.

• Explain that when they complete the task, they should clean up the station so it looks like it did before they began work. Tell them to let you know if they need any materials as they work, including a sharpened pencil.

• Be sure students find the numbers of their stations on the answer sheets before beginning.

Electricity Assessment *(cont.)*

Task 1

Connect the wire, battery, and bulb to light the bulb. Draw a diagram to show how you did this and label the parts of your drawing. Be sure to use large dots to show where the connections are between the parts.

Now, find three more ways to connect the parts to make the bulb light and draw them.

Task 2

Construct a conductor tester from the materials at this table and test the items for conductivity. Draw what your conductor tester looks like.

Conductor Tester

List the materials which conducted electricity and made the bulb work.

_____ _____

_____ _____

_____ _____

_____ _____

_____ _____

Write a sentence which tells what you found about conductors of electricity.

_____

_____

Give an example of something else which would conduct electricity but is not with the materials at this table. _____

Electricity Assessment *(cont.)*

Task 3

Construct a conductor tester from the materials on the table and then check to find where the connections are between the brads in this box lid. Record your test in the box on the left.

Connect the numbers to show which made the light of the tester work.

```
┌─────────────────┐
│  1       5      │
│                 │
│  2       6      │
│                 │
│  3       7      │
│                 │
│  4       8      │
└─────────────────┘
```

Remove the cover from the box lid. Draw where the wires are connected to the brads.

```
┌─────────────────┐
│  1       5      │
│                 │
│  2       6      │
│                 │
│  3       7      │
│                 │
│  4       8      │
└─────────────────┘
```

Which brads made the tester light work but were not connected by wire? _____

Explain how the electricity could go between these brads even though they did not have a wire connecting them. _____

Task 4

Look at the circuits shown below and decide if they will work. If they will, circle **Y**; if not, circle **N**. Draw the changes needed to make the circuits work where you circled **N**.

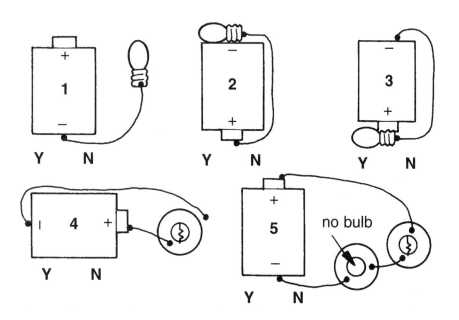

Teacher and Student Resources

Related Books

Cole, Joanna. *The Magic School Bus® and the Electric Field Trip.* Scholastic Press, 1997. The students in Ms. Frizzle's class take another fantastic journey, this time through a power plant. Along the way they learn about magnetism, static, and current electricity.

Macaulay, David. *The Way Things Work.* Houghton Mifflin Co., 1988. This book is filled with humorous cartoons which offer simple explanations for how things work, including electric motors, light bulbs, batteries, and magnets.

Sneider, Cary, A. Gould, and B. Wentz, *The "Magic" of Electricity: A School Assembly Program Grades 3–6* may be ordered online at **http://www.lhs.berkeley.edu/GEMS/gemsguides.html**

This Great Explorations in Math and Science (GEMS) Assembly Presenter's Guide provides sample scripts and instructions for an assembly program that can educate and entertain several hundred students at a time, with a high degree of audience participation. In an hour-long session thoroughly described in this book, the student-audience takes part in impressive demonstrations by the "Wizard of Electricity." Students distinguish "magic" from science as volunteers help the Wizard create electricity. (Slides for this program may be ordered separately.)

Young, Ruth. Science Literature Unit: *The Magic School Bus® and the Electric Field Trip.* Teacher Created Resources, Inc., 1999. **http://www.teachercreated.com/**

This book is filled with hands-on activities which bring to life the adventures of Ms. Frizzle's students in Joanna Cole's book (see above).

Suppliers of Science Materials:

Delta Education (800) 282-9560 Request a catalog of materials or order online at their Web site. **http://www.delta-education.com/corp/info/search.html**

Supplies a wide variety of science and math materials, including assorted magnets, small light bulbs, bulb and battery holders.

National Science Resource Center **http://www.si.edu/nsrc/**

Resources for Teaching Elementary Science. National Science Resource Center, National Academy Press, Washington, D.C., 1996. This outstanding resource guide to hands-on inquiry-centered elementary science curriculum materials and resources. Each reference in this guide has been carefully evaluated and is fully described, including addresses.

Read this book online or order it from **http://www.nap.edu/catalog/4966.html**

National Science Teachers Association(NSTA) (800) 277-5300

http://www.nsta.org/ or the online catalog of materials at **http://store.nsta.org/**

Provides books, posters, and software related to astronomy and other sciences.

A monthly professional journal, the bimonthly NSTA Reports, discounts at the regional and national conventions, and an annual catalog of materials are all available.